Mahatma Gandhi

Jennifer Strand

abdopublishing.com

Published by Abdo Zoom™, PO Box 398166, Minneapolis, Minnesota 55439. Copyright © 2017 by Abdo Consulting Group, Inc. International copyrights reserved in all countries. No part of this book may be reproduced in any form without written permission from the publisher. Abdo Zoom™ is a trademark and logo of Abdo Consulting Group, Inc.

Printed in the United States of America, North Mankato, Minnesota
072016
092016

THIS BOOK CONTAINS
RECYCLED MATERIALS

Cover Photo: AP Images
Interior Photos: AP Images, 1, 5, 7, 10; Rex Features/AP Images, 4; World History Archive/Newscom, 9; Dinodia Photos/Getty Images, 8–9; Wallace Kirkland/The LIFE Picture Collection/Getty Images, 12; W. Bossard/Deutscher Photo Dienst/AP Images, 13; VCG Wilson/Bettmann Archive/Getty Images, 14–15; Bettmann/Getty Images, 16; Keystone/Stringer/Getty Images, 18–19

Editor: Brienna Rossiter
Series Designer: Madeline Berger
Art Direction: Dorothy Toth

Publisher's Cataloging-in-Publication Data
Names: Strand, Jennifer, author.
Title: Mahatma Gandhi / by Jennifer Strand.
Description: Minneapolis, MN : Abdo Zoom, [2017] | Series: Legendary leaders
    | Includes bibliographical references and index.
Identifiers: LCCN 2016941381 | ISBN 9781680792386 (lib. bdg.) |
    ISBN 9781680794069 (ebook) | 9781680794953 (Read-to-me ebook)
Subjects: LCSH: Gandhi, Mahatma, 1869-1948--Juvenile literature. | Nationalists-
    -India--Biography--Juvenile literature. | Statesmen--India--Biography--
    Juvenile literature. | Pacifists--India--Biography--Juvenile literature. |
    Nonviolence--India--History--20th century--Juvenile literature. | India
    Politics and government--1919-1947--Juvenile literature.
Classification: DDC 954.03/5092 [B]--dc23
LC record available at http://lccn.loc.gov/2016941381

Table of Contents

Introduction. 4

Early Life. 6

Leader. 8

History Maker 12

Legacy. 16

Quick Stats. 20

Key Dates 21

Glossary 22

Booklinks 23

Index 24

Mohandas Gandhi led peaceful protests.

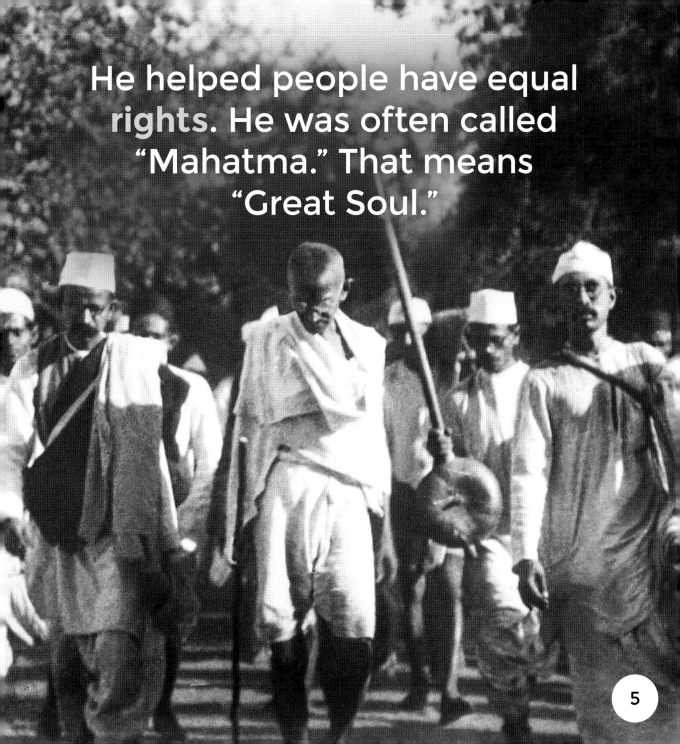

He helped people have equal rights. He was often called "Mahatma." That means "Great Soul."

5

Early Life

Mohandas was born on October 2, 1869. He lived in India. He was shy. But he was always thinking.

Leader

Gandhi went to South Africa. Indian people there were treated unfairly.

Gandhi led a protest. It helped Indian people get equal rights.

Later he returned
to India.

The British ruled India. They were not always fair. Many Indian people wanted to be free.

Gandhi wanted to help.
He led protests.

12

He asked people to disobey unfair laws. They stopped paying **taxes**, too.

Gandhi also met with British leaders. They gave Indian people more freedom.

India became independent in 1947.

Legacy

Gandhi helped people get equal rights. But some people did not like his ideas. He was killed on January 30, 1948.

People around
the world admired
him. Many leaders
used his ideas.

They led peaceful protests, too.

Mahatma Gandhi

Born: October 2, 1869

Birthplace: Porbandar, Gujarat, India

Known For: Gandhi was a civil rights leader. He led peaceful protests in India and South Africa.

Died: January 30, 1948

Key Dates

1869: Mohandas Karamchand Gandhi is born on October 2.

1893: Gandhi goes to South Africa and leads a protest.

1915: Gandhi returns to India.

1920: Gandhi becomes president of a group that works for India's independence.

1947: India gains independence from Great Britain.

1948: Gandhi is killed on January 30.

Glossary

independent - not ruled or controlled by another person or country.

protest - an event where people show they oppose something.

rights - the things that people can do under the law.

taxes - money that people pay to the government in return for services, such as police and roads.

Booklinks

For more information
on **Mahatma Gandhi**, please visit
booklinks.abdopublishing.com

Zoom In on Biographies!

Learn even more with the Abdo Zoom
Biographies database. Check out
abdozoom.com for more information.

Index

born, 6

British, 11, 14

independent, 15

India, 6, 10, 11, 15

Indian people, 8,
9, 11, 14

killed, 17

peaceful, 4, 19

protests, 4, 9,
12, 19

rights, 5, 9, 17

South Africa, 8

taxes, 13